1000 Years of Scottish Chu
Mid nineteenth century churc
the Disruption to the Restoration of the
Roman Catholic Hierarchy, 1843 to 1878

John R. Hume

Isle of Whithorn Free Church

© John R. Hume, 2018
First published in the United Kingdom, 2018,
by Stenlake Publishing Ltd.
www.stenlake.co.uk
ISBN 978-1-84033-814-0

The publishers regret that they cannot supply
copies of any pictures featured in this book.

Printed by
Berforts, 17 Burgess Road, Hastings, TN35 4NR

Dedication

To everyone who has been responsible for the creation and maintenance of church buildings
in Scotland over the last 1000 years

Acknowledgements

My prime acknowledgement is to my family, my wife Hope and my sons
Matthew, Kenneth, Peter and Colin for their support over many years, and my
father William Hume who introduced me to churches of a wide variety of
denominations: without them this series of books could not have been written

Over a lifetime of involvement with church buildings I have cause to thank the
many people who have given me insights both into individual congregations and
into church organisation. I am particularly grateful to the Church of Scotland for
periods of service as an Advisory Member of the General Trustees and as a
member of the Committee on Artistic Matters (now the Committee on Church Art
and Architecture). While I worked with what is now Historic Environment
Scotland as an Inspector of Ancient Monuments, and subsequently as an Inspector
of Historic Buildings I had opportunities to visit many of the buildings included
here. I am also very grateful to the staff of Historic Environment Scotland, and
particularly Veronica Fraser, for supplying me with digital copies of some of my
photographs.

As a founder member of Scotland's Churches Scheme and as a Trustee both of
that body and of its successor, the Scotland's Churches Trust, I have developed a
knowledge of the church estate throughout Scotland which in a very direct way
prepared the way for putting together this series. I am most grateful to my
colleagues on both bodies.

It would be invidious to single out a few of the many individuals who have
helped, but I feel that I must mention the late Frank Lawrie, my superior officer in
Historic Scotland, who was very supportive of my work with churches. I would also
like to thank Stenlake Publishing for undertaking the publication of this series, and
the staff of the Mitchell Library, Glasgow for their assistance over the years.

Finally, I hope that my many friends in church and architectural circles will
realise that they are all included in these expressions of gratitude.

Further Reading

There are many histories of individual churches in Scotland,
variable in quality, but none negligible. Most of them concentrate,
understandably, on congregational life, and often say very little
about church buildings, but all are worth reading to build up a
rounded history of the Church in Scotland. In the preparation of this
series of volumes I have found the following more comprehensive
books particularly useful:

Ewing, The Rev W, *Annals of the Free Church of Scotland*, T and
T Clark, Edinburgh, 1914
Groome, FH (ed), *An Ordnance Gazetteer of Scotland*, 2nd edn,
William Mackenzie, Edinburgh and London, c1895
Hay, G, *The Architecture of Scottish Post-Reformation Churches, 1560-
1843*, Oxford University Press, 1957
Hume, JR, *Scotland's Best Churches*, Edinburgh University Press, 2005
Lamb, The Rev JA (ed) and Macdonald, *The Rev FAJ (ed), Fasti
Ecclesiae Scotticanae: Ministers of the Church of Scotland, vols I-XI*,
various publishers and dates
Lamb, The Rev JA (ed), *The Fasti of the United Free Church of Scotland,
1900-1929*, Oliver and Boyd, Edinburgh, 1956
Small, The Rev R, *Congregations of the United Presbyterian Church,
1733-1900*, David M Small, Edinburgh, 1904
Various authors and publishers, *The Buildings of Scotland* and The Royal
Incorporation of Architects in Scotland *Architectural Guides* series.

Also the Sacred Scotland series of handbooks and other publications of
the Scotland's Churches Scheme and the Scotland's Churches Trust.

Series Introduction

The oldest churches in Scotland for which we have firm above-ground evidence appear to date from the early-mid-11th century. Before that, however, there were probably wooden churches, as found in excavations at Whithorn. There are also the round towers at Brechin, Abernethy and Egilsay which may be earlier than the earliest surviving parts of stone churches. The establishment of focal points for Christian worship probably pre-dates the construction of church buildings, and many of the surviving free-standing sculptured crosses may have been intended for that purpose. Good examples of such crosses can be seen at Aberlemno, Glamis and Logierait in southern Pictland, and at Nigg, Shandwick and Hilton of Cadboll in northern Pictland. In what was Gaelic Scotland there are fine crosses at Kildalton, Islay and on Iona, while in the cradle of Christianity in Wigtownshire there are crosses in the Whithorn Museum and in the parish church of Kirkinner which probably fulfilled a similar role. This practice of marking 'sacred places' with stone monuments can probably be traced back from early Christianity into the Bronze Age and the Neolithic period.

The purpose of this series of volumes is not, however, to engage in debate, scholarly or otherwise, so it is fair to assume that the earliest roofed stone Christian churches are about a thousand years old. In the lecture I gave in 2014 for the Scotland's Churches Trust, I showed photographs of about 100 churches from the 11th to the 21st centuries, mostly existing buildings, but including some demolished during the past half-century or so. In preparing this series I have drawn on the material collected for that lecture, but have supplemented it by including many more churches which shed light, for one reason or another, on changes in church organisation, worship practice and architectural fashion over the millennium concerned. The original choice of buildings was explicitly personal: churches with a particular meaning for me by virtue of aesthetic appeal or association, or both. I have carried this through into the present collection, which also takes account of geographical and denominational diversity. This will, I hope, not be considered egotism: it is just that I believe that I cannot write honourably or convincingly in this context about buildings that do not have some real meaning for me. A handful, however, have been included because they 'ought' to be there; I will not identify them. A few years ago I wrote a book entitled *Scotland's Best Churches*, which concentrated on churches then in use. Here I have included churches not in use as such, roofless and ruined buildings, parts of buildings, and some now demolished. I have endeavoured to present a balanced selection of churches of different periods, denominations and architectural styles. In captioning I have concentrated on highlighting particular points of interest relating to the images, rather than giving 'potted histories' of the buildings concerned. The number of changes in the names of churches over the years has made it impossible to include them all; in a few instances I have included more than one. As far as possible the first name quoted is the original one. The assigning of dates is very difficult. I have chosen to list churches by date of completion rather than date of design or commencement of construction. I have used my judgement in interpreting the various dates to be found in published sources. Because old counties were an important context for church building I have used them in headings; modern local authority areas are not notably helpful.

Finally, please do not look on this collection as a work of scholarship (though I have done my best to make it scholarly). Look on it, rather, as a love-letter to the Church Universal. Each of these buildings is in its own way a place to encounter God, Father, Son and Holy Spirit, and to go out into the world imbued with the idea of loving God and loving our neighbours.

John R Hume
Glasgow
March 2018

Sustaining Scotland's places of worship.
15 North Bank Street, Edinburgh, EH1 2LP
0131 225 8644
Registered Charity: SC043105

From the Disruption to the Restoration of the Roman Catholic Hierarchy in 1878

The outside dates of this section are each in its own way of compelling importance not only to Scotland's church history but also to the people of the country. In the last volume I referred to the creation of the Free Church as a breakaway from the Established Church. The end year of this period was when the Roman Catholic Hierarchy was officially restored, with bishops and archbishops consecrated to serve as spiritual and administrative leaders of the dioceses which covered the country for the first time (in Roman Catholic terms) since the Reformation. This legitimation of what had become a major denomination, as a result of large-scale migration from Ireland since the 1840s, reflected a growing tolerance of religious difference. Between 1843 and 1878 changes had taken place in Scotland which were important in the development of the Free, Roman Catholic and Scottish Episcopal churches, and of the new United Presbyterian Church formed in 1847 by a union of the United Associate Synod and the Relief Church. These began, in fact, in 1840 with the introduction of the Penny Post, and continued sequentially with the introduction of a national network of electric telegraphy, the creation of an interlinked network of steamboat and railway transport covering most of Scotland, and the development of both book and newspaper printing. All of these speeded up the transfer of ideas, as well as of news, and allowed people to move around the country on an unprecedented scale.

As far as church building was concerned the towns and cities continued to expand rapidly, and so, too, were the populations of the more fertile areas of agricultural land. Mechanisation of stone-working, brick-making and woodworking, the increasing availability of good-quality imported timber and glass and improvements in iron and steel production and iron-founding all made the construction of churches cheaper. A further stimulus to church-building was competition for members and esteem, especially among the three major Presbyterian denominations.

In design terms the most obvious trend was the increasing adoption of the Gothic Revival as the preferred style. This was strongly influenced by AWN Pugin, who asserted that the Gothic was the only true Christian style. The United Presbyterian and Free churches, however, continued to build Classical buildings. The Scottish Episcopal Church was much influenced by the Oxford Movement in the Church of England, which advocated a return to pre-Reformation liturgical worship, and many small and a few large Episcopal churches were constructed in these middle decades of the 19th century. St Ninian's Episcopal Cathedral in Perth was the first cathedral in Britain to be started since the Reformation.

Note: **D** after a caption means demolished: **A** means adapted to other uses or disused

Steeple of Strathaven Relief Church (Strathaven East Parish Church), Lanarkshire

The first part of this building was constructed in 1777 as a Relief church. The tower and steeple were added in 1843, and the body of the church was enlarged in 1877 by the United Presbyterian congregation which had succeeded the Relief one in 1847. This steeple was one of the first built for a Secession congregation. The church is a notable feature of central Strathaven.

Skirling Free Church, Peebles-shire

The Disruption in the Church of Scotland in 1843 was rapidly followed by the building of new churches for the congregations which had left. This is a detail of Skirling Free, a village church built in the Disruption year. **A**

St Sylvester's Roman Catholic Church, Elgin, Moray
This elegant little church was built in 1843 and designed by Thomas Mackenzie in association with the Rt Rev James Kyle, as part of the latter's programme of repopulating north-east Scotland with Roman Catholic churches.

St Mary's Scottish Episcopal Church, Dalkeith, Midlothian
This little building was constructed in 1843 as a private chapel for Dalkeith Palace. It was designed by William Burn and David Bryce. It is now the Scottish Episcopal church for the town of Dalkeith.

The Triple Kirks, Aberdeen
In the immediate aftermath of the Disruption a large Free church was built in central Aberdeen to accommodate three congregations which had left the Church of Scotland. The new building was cheaply built of brick to a design by Archibald Simpson. It is on the left in this view, with the Trades' Hall in front of it. The church in the middle is a Congregational church constructed in 1865. **A**

Alyth Free Church, Perthshire

This church was built in 1843 for a congregation which had left the recently-built parish church. Alyth was a textile town at the time. The simplicity of this design was typical of many early Free churches.

A

Isle of Whithorn Free Church, Wigtownshire

This is another early Free church, constructed in 1843-44. No site in this little port could be obtained, so it was built on land reclaimed from the seashore.

The steeple of the Assembly Hall of the Church of Scotland (Tolbooth Church), Edinburgh

This building was constructed between 1839 and 1844 to a design by James Gillespie Graham and AWN Pugin as a hall in which to hold the General Assembly of the Church of Scotland. By the time it was completed this Church had split. It remained the Assembly Hall until 1929, when the United Free Church merged with the Church of Scotland. It also functioned as the Tolbooth Parish Church. The steeple is seen here towering over buildings in Victoria Street.

A

Glenfincastle Free Church (Glenfincastle Chapel), Perthshire

Glenfincastle is in a remote part of Highland Perthshire. This deliberately picturesque little building was built as a Free church in 1843-44.

Banff Free Church (Trinity and Alvah Parish Church), Banffshire

Not all early Free churches were modest structures. This one is splendidly Classical, with a finely-detailed cupola, and is a prominent feature of the attractive county town of Banffshire. It was designed by James and Robert Raeburn and built in 1834-44, immediately after the Disruption.

Edinburgh Catholic Apostolic Church

The Catholic Apostolic Church was founded in the 1820s by a Church of Scotland minister, the Rev Edward Irving. It was notably unorthodox in its beliefs and worship practices. This building was constructed between 1843 and 1844 for Mr Irving, possibly to designs by John Dick Peddie. **A**

Reay Free Church, Shebster, Caithness
This is an unusual design of Free church, one of two in north Caithness of this type, with two parallel roofs. This one served a rural area and was built in 1844. **A**

Ayr Free Church (Sandgate Parish Church), Ayrshire
In the newly fashionable Romanesque style, this church was, like that in Banff, constructed in the centre of a county town, a gesture of confidence by the new Free Church. It was designed by William Gale and built in 1844-45. **A**

Millburn Free Church, Renton, Dunbartonshire

The congregation which built this church began as a mission in 1844 to this important calico-printing town. Distinguished by its remarkably elaborate spire, it was built in 1844-45, and probably designed by the Glasgow architect JT Rochhead, whose St John's Free Church in Glasgow had a comparable, but larger steeple. **A**

Loudoun Parish Church, Newmilns, Ayrshire
The long-established Ayrshire fashion of building churches with Classical steeples reached a conclusion with this one, whose steeple is unusually slender. The designer was James Ingram of Kilmarnock, and it was constructed in 1844-45, for a hand-loom weaving village.

St Mary's Roman Catholic Chapel, Hamilton
This was the second post-Reformation Roman Catholic chapel built in Lanarkshire, following St Margaret's, Airdrie. St Mary's was built in 1846 to serve a growing population of Irish Catholic immigrants, fleeing the Potato Famine.

Newmilns Free Church (Newmilns Loudoun East Parish Church)

A singularly neat little church, this building was constructed in 1846 for a congregation which had left Loudoun Parish Church at the Disruption. The steepled belfry is an echo of the Ayrshire tradition of Classical steeples. **D**

Kiltarlity Free Church, Inverness-shire

Kiltarlity is a village in rural Inverness-shire, and this Free church, built in 1843-46 represents a very basic approach to church design. With its plain rectangular windows and simple belfry it could well have been constructed in the mid-18th century. It is moving in its uncompromising form.

Fort William Free Church, Inverness-shire
Fort William, originally founded as a garrison town, had by the mid-19th century become a market town for a large part of western Inverness-shire. This Free church of 1846 is appropriately more elaborate than Kiltarlity.

Alexandria United Associate Church (Vale of Leven Baptist Church), Dunbartonshire

The congregation which built this pleasingly simple Classical church in 1847 began as part of the Relief Church, but for complex reasons had become by that time part of the United Associate Church. The building was completed immediately before the United Associate and Relief churches came together as the United Presbyterian Church.

Bannockburn Free Church (Murrayfield United Free Church), Stirlingshire

This was originally built as a plain rectangular building in 1849-50 to designs by James Harley. The tower was added in 1853, on the lines of an earlier 19th century building.

Arrochar Parish Church, Dunbartonshire

Arrochar is a little village at the head of Loch Long, which expanded in the first half of the 19th century with the development of steamboat services. This church was built for the Church of Scotland in 1845-47 to replace an earlier building, the remains of which still survive. The new building was designed by Glasgow architect William Spence.

Duns United Presbyterian Church (Duns South Parish Church), Berwickshire

The congregation of this very neat little church was established in 1763 as a Secession church. It was rebuilt into this form in 1851. Duns is a Borders market town for a rich agricultural area.   **A**

Rhu Parish Church (Rhu and Shandon Parish Church), Dunbartonshire

This building was constructed in 1851 to replace a church of 1763, and was designed, like Arrochar, by William Spence of Glasgow. The new church was built partly at the expense of Robert Napier, the 'father of Clyde shipbuilding', who had a mansion in the parish. The church was extended to the rear in 1891 by Honeyman and Keppie.

Renfield St Stephen's Parish Church, Glasgow

In the late 1840s 'correct' Gothic Revival churches, based on mediaeval English and French models, began to be built in Scotland. This is one of the first, constructed in 1849-52 for an Independent congregation to designs by JT Emmett, a London architect. The steeple in this view was recently rebuilt after it collapsed in a gale.

St Columba's Scottish Episcopal Church, Poltalloch, Argyll

This is another 'correct' Gothic Revival building, originally built as an estate chapel for Poltalloch House, in mid-Argyll. It was built in 1852-54, and designed by Thomas Cundy, a London architect.

St Paul's Scottish Episcopal Church (St Paul's Scottish Episcopal Cathedral), Dundee

This dramatic building is in the centre of Dundee, and was built in 1852-55 as a gesture of confidence in the revival of the Scottish Episcopal Church, to a design by George Gilbert Scott, the leading English architect of the period. It was made the cathedral of the Diocese of Brechin in 1905.

The West Parish Church (Westburn Parish Church), Greenock, Renfrewshire

The construction in 1839-41 of the body of this church in the West End of Greenock has already been referred to. This view is included to show the soaring beauty of the Classical steeple added in 1855, the last of its kind to be built in Scotland.

Burray United Presbyterian Church (The Parish Church of St Lawrence), Orkney

At the other extreme of 1850s church design, this little, very basic, building is on Burray, one of the south isles of Orkney, and was constructed in 1856. **A**

The East Free Church (Brechin Baptist Church), Brechin, Angus

This large Gothic Revival Free church was built in 1855-56 to designs by JW and JM Hay, Liverpool architects. The entrance through the base of the tower is characteristic of their work. **A**

Elgin Place Congregational Church, Glasgow
Though the Gothic Revival was favoured by congregations of several denominations, the rationality and dignity of the Classical appealed to others. This large and dignified building was constructed in 1855-56, and was designed by John Burnet. **D**

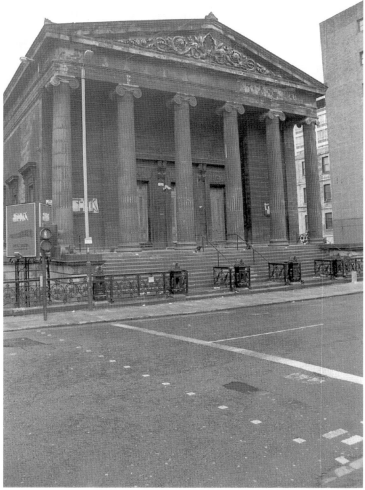

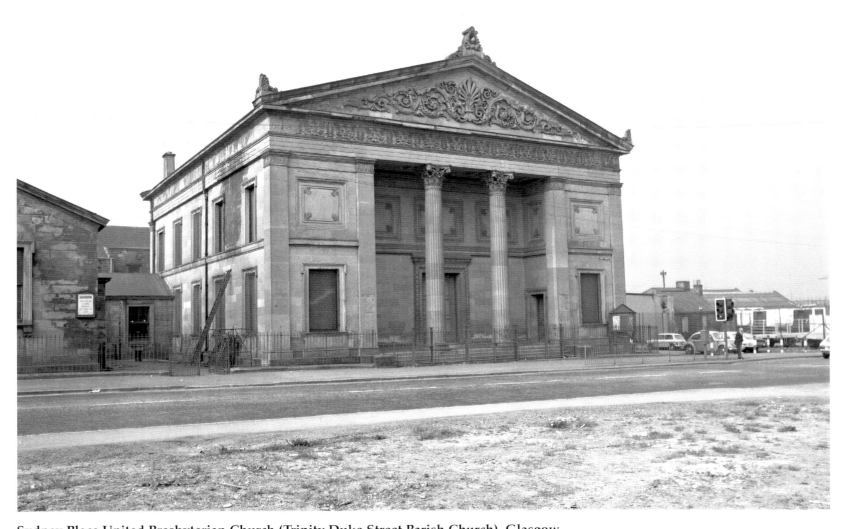

Sydney Place United Presbyterian Church (Trinity Duke Street Parish Church), Glasgow
Back to the Glasgow Classical, this time for a United Presbyterian congregation originally founded as a Burgher congregation in East Campbell Street in 1789. This elegant church dates from 1857-58 and was designed by Edinburgh architects Peddie and Kinnear.

A

Invergordon Free Church (Invergordon Parish Church), Ross and Cromarty

This is one of a series of large Gothic Revival Free churches built in Easter Ross from the late 1850s, and is probably the finest of them. Designed by the Inverness firm of Ross and Joass, the Invergordon one was built in 1859-61, and is the centrepiece of the town and a notable land- and sea-mark.

St Mary's Scottish Episcopal Church, Birnam, Perthshire

The village of Birnam grew up from the 1850s when a railway from Perth was opened. This brought summer visitors, and this little church was built between 1856 and 1858 to accommodate them. The church was designed by William Slater. The top of the tower was added in 1870.

St Vincent Street United Presbyterian Church (St Vincent Street Parish Church), Glasgow

Back to Glasgow classicism, but with a difference, this church was designed by Alexander 'Greek' Thomson for a hillside setting and built in 1857-59. The powerfully temple-like body of the church, with hall accommodation underneath, is given unusual vertical emphasis by Thomson's tower, in a mixture of Greek and Egyptian styles.

John Street United Presbyterian Church (John Street Parish Church), Glasgow
Set in the heart of Glasgow's 'Merchant City', Classical, but not orthodox in treatment, John Street was designed by JT Rochhead, and was opened in 1860. Like St Vincent Street it had halls on the ground floor, but is clearly a street-frontage building, with the dynamic that entails. It was built on the site of a Relief church constructed in 1793. **A**

Renfrew Parish Church (Renfrew Old Parish Church), Renfrewshire

This supremely elegant and dignified Gothic Revival church was constructed in 1861-62 to a design by JT Rochhead, incorporating fragments from a mediaeval predecessor. Other, very different, Rochhead churches have already been included, Millburn Free, Renton and John Street, Glasgow. **A**

Tighnabruaich Free Church, Argyll.

Like Arrochar, Tighnabruaich developed as a resort because of steamboat services. This very pleasing and characterful little church was built in 1863, and was designed by Boucher and Cousland. **D**

Penicuik Free Church (Penicuik South Parish Church), Midlothian

Alexander Thomson and JT Rochhead broke away from convention in their interpretations of the Classical, and FT Pilkington took similar liberties with the Gothic. This church was built in 1862 for the paper-making town of Penicuik, where Pilkington had developed a friendship with the largest local paper-makers, the Cowan family. The complex form of this building is obvious in this views, but not the richly-carved detailing.

Kelvinside Free Church (Kelvinside Parish Church), Glasgow
The inspiration for this striking building, designed by JJ Stevenson of Campbell Douglas and Stevenson, was unusually German Gothic. It was built in 1862, and these views show it soon after completion. It is now hemmed in by other buildings, and the essence of the design can no longer be appreciated.
                                                                                    A

Lansdowne United Presbyterian Church (Lansdowne Parish Church), Glasgow
A short walk away from the last church, Lansdowne (built 1862-63) was an offshoot from Cambridge Street United Presbyterian Church in the centre of Glasgow, and was intended to serve the wealthy West End of the city. It is on Great Western Road, and its spire, the tallest in Glasgow, was designed as an 'eye catcher' by the architect, John Honeyman.　**A**

Irvine United Presbyterian Church (Irvine Trinity Parish Church), Ayrshire
This is FT Pilkington's first large church, built between 1861 and 1863. When it was built it stood on a prominent site in Irvine, looking over the River Irvine. Its abnormally tall spire was a dominant feature of the town, but its impact has been much reduced by the construction of a massive retail centre over the river. It is now very difficult to photograph. These views show the river frontage, with the striking use of white and red sandstone for dramatic effect clearly evident. **A**

St Mary's Scottish Episcopal Church, Aberdeen
St Mary's is another example of the use of stones of different colours, in this case grey and pink granites. Roof tiles of different colours in geometric patterns are also used, giving rise to the local nickname 'The Tartan Kirkie'. It was built in 1862-64 and designed by the Rev FG Lee and Alexander Ellis in 'Scottish-Italian Gothic'. The chancel, on the right was damaged during the Second World War, and repaired in 1950-51 by John Alistair Ross.

All Saints' Scottish Episcopal Church, Kinlochrannoch, Perthshire

Kinlochrannoch is a remote village in Highland Perthshire. This little church was designed by Andrew Heiton, junior, of Perth and built in 1864. He has given distinction to an otherwise unremarkable building by the slated spire and belfry.

Facing page left:
East Campbell Street United Presbyterian Church, Glasgow

After these exotic church designs it is refreshing to see such a dignified 'flat-Classical' building as this church in the East End of Glasgow. It was constructed in 1863-64 and designed by Haig and Low to replace a Relief church of 1792.

Facing page right:
The Barclay Free Church (Barclay Viewforth Parish Church), Edinburgh

This is FT Pilkington's most spectacular church, built in 1862-64 on restricted site in Bruntsfield, in the south-west of Edinburgh. Not all the carvings were completed, but the uncarved blocks have an appeal of their own.

Dowanhill Free Church (Dowanhill Parish Church), Glasgow

This imposing church, on an elevated corner site in Glasgow's West End, was built in 1863-65 in French Gothic style. It was designed by William Leiper, an up-and-coming young architect, with a spectacular interior. **A**

Hope Park United Free Church (Hope Park and Martyrs Parish Church), St Andrews, Fife

Much less 'correct' Gothic than Dowanhill or Lansdowne churches in Glasgow, Hope Park was designed by Peddie and Kinnear of Edinburgh and built in 1864-65. The large rose window had by that time become emblematic of the United Presbyterians.

Kelso North Free Church (Kelso North Parish Church), Roxburghshire

This was FT Pilkington's last church, conventional in overall form, but with the full range of the architect's idiosyncratic detailing. It was built in 1865-67.

Bellanoch Free Church, Argyll

To cleanse the palate I include here a church of the simplest character, at Bellanoch, above the Crinan Canal in mid-Argyll. The pointed windows are the only 'ornament' in this little building constructed in 1868-69.

Dingwall Free Church, Ross and Cromarty

This is another of the large Free churches in Easter Ross, one of the heartlands of the denomination. The unusual cupola on this building was constructed instead of an intended spire, giving the church a very distinctive profile. It was built between 1867 and 1870, and designed by John Rhind.

Rosskeen Free Church, Ross and Cromarty

This stylish Free church is set in open country close to the Cromarty Firth. The clear east-coast light emphasises the careful balance of the design. It was built in about 1870.

Peaton Church, Coulport, Dunbartonshire

Corrugated-iron was much used in the later 19th century and the early 20th century both for temporary churches and for small country churches. This one was constructed in 1870 as a mission church in an area becoming popular with summer residents, and is unusually elegant.

The West Free Church (St Matthew's Parish Church), Perth

This building, with its dominant spire, was specifically designed to be a prominent riverside feature in Perth. The church was designed by John Honeyman of Glasgow, architect of Lansdowne Church, Glasgow, and was constructed between 1869 and 1871.

The Middle Free Church (St George's North Parish Church), Greenock, Renfrewshire

The tall steeple of this church was also designed as an eye-catcher, at the east end of Union Street, in the fashionable West End of Greenock. The church was designed by Salmon, Son and Ritchie of Glasgow, and built in 1870-71. The top of the steeple appears to have been modelled on that of St George's Tron Church in Glasgow.					**A**

West Linton Parish Church, Peebles-shire

Originally built in 1781-82, incorporating mediaeval stonework, this church was substantially remodelled in 1871. The steeple dates from that reconstruction, which created a very attractive effect, as seen here.

Door-head, Trinity United Presbyterian Church (Ardgowan Parish Church, now part of the Lyle Kirk), Greenock, Renfrewshire
This church was built in 1871 to designs by John Starforth, not far from the Middle United Presbyterian Church. It is in Gothic Revival style, with a substantial tower. Its most attractive feature is, however, this door-head (tympanum), with floriated carving and in the centre two angels with a bible, under a canopy.

Claremont Methodist Church, Glasgow

The largest and most elaborate Methodist church in Glasgow, this building was constructed in about 1871-73 to serve the Finnieston area to the west of the city centre. In 'flat-Classical' style. There is a comparable church in Cowcaddens, formerly St Stephen's, now the Scottish Piping Centre, designed by Campbell Douglas and Sellars, who were probably also the architects of the Claremont building. **D**

St Kilda's Scottish Episcopal Church, Lochbuie, Isle of Mull, Argyll

This tiny church was built in 1874 in the south of the Isle of Mull, as a private chapel for a local landowner, in a fine landscape setting.

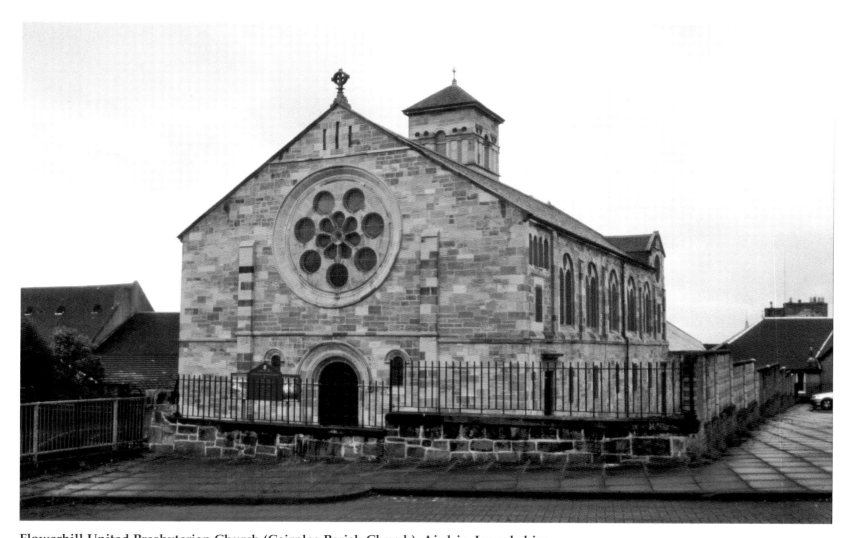

Flowerhill United Presbyterian Church (Cairnlea Parish Church), Airdrie, Lanarkshire
This church was built in 1873 by a Reformed Presbyterian congregation, which joined the Church of Scotland in that year, becoming Flowerhill Chapel of Ease. It became a quoad sacra parish church in 1875.

Birsay Free Church (Twatt Parish Church), Twatt, Orkney
Birsay Free is a large but plain building set in a tree-less landscape towards the west side of the Mainland of Orkney. Built in 1874, it suits suits its environment perfectly.
A

Palmerston Place United Free Church (Palmerston Place Parish Church), Edinburgh
This remarkable Italianate church in Edinburgh's West End was constructed in 1873-75 for the congregation of Rose Street Chapel, a former Secession church. The new building was designed by Peddie and Kinnear, and is still a very striking piece of streetscape.

St Fillan's Scottish Episcopal Church, Killin, Perthshire

This is another corrugated-iron church. The oldest part, nearest to the road, was built as a private chapel by the 7th Earl of Breadalbane in 1876. It was extended to the east (right) in the early 20th century. St Fillan was a local saint.

The Leckie Memorial United Presbyterian Church (St Andrew's Leckie Parish Church, Peebles, Peebles-shire

By the 1870s Peebles was a popular place for retirement and holidays, as well as being a centre for woollen manufacture. This church was built in 1875-77 to designs by Peddie and Kinnear on a site overlooking the River Tweed. The congregation came from a former Burgher Secession church in the town, whose minister from 1794 was the Rev Mr Leckie.

Strathaven East United Free Church (Strathaven East Parish Church), Lanarkshire

The spire of this church, built in 1843, has already been noticed. As mentioned there, the body of the building was constructed in 1777 as Strathaven Relief Church. This view shows the church as it appeared in 1877, after it had been enlarged. It is a striking feature in the park at the centre of this little town.

The Parish Church of St Nicholas (St Nicholas Uniting Church), Aberdeen

The West Church here has already been mentioned. The East Church, right in this view, was rebuilt in 1835-37 to designs by Archibald Simpson, as was the south transept, on the left. A fire in 1874 gutted the East Church and destroyed the lead-covered wooden steeple. The tower and steeple seen here were designed by W and J Smith, and constructed in 1875-80.

Adelaide Place Baptist Church, Glasgow

This is Glasgow's largest Baptist church, in Blythswood to the west of the city centre. It was built in 1875-77 to designs by TL Watson.

Rosehall United Presbyterian Church (Priestfield Parish Church), Edinburgh

In the south side of Edinburgh, this church is in Lombardic Gothic (in fact Romanesque) style, briefly popular in the Edinburgh area in the 1870s. This is the largest and finest Scottish church built in that style. It was designed by Sutherland and Walker, and built in 1878-80 for a congregation formed in 1878 in temporary premises.